Emergency Preparedness for Federal Employees in the National Capital Region

FEMA P-912 / September 2012

Contents

FEMA

As Federal employees, we all have a range of responsibilities: to our families, loved ones, communities, and the American public. By preparing for emergencies, we can enhance the safety of our families and strengthen our ability to carry out our work.

This guide was produced by the FEMA Office of National Capital Region Coordination to encourage Federal employees and the whole community in the Washington, D.C. area to take practical steps to better prepare ourselves and our families for emergencies that could threaten our homes, workplaces, and communities.

We all have a role to play in serving our nation and keeping ourselves and our families safe. I encourage you to review this guide and take these important steps so you and your family will be better prepared for an emergency or unexpected crisis.

We would like to thank the U.S. Office of Personnel Management and all of our regional partners for their continued support in preparing the Federal workforce in the National Capital Region.

Sincerely,

Steward D. Beckham
Director
Office of National Capital Region Coordination
Federal Emergency Management Agency
U.S. Department of Homeland Security

Each day, you and other Federal employees provide an array of essential services. Your own personal readiness for natural, accidental, or intentional hazards is a key part of the Federal Government's ability to continue serving its citizens.

Emergencies can happen at any time, without warning. Federal, State, local, and non governmental organizations are committed to helping people in need, but that assistance may be delayed during a large incident. You and your family should be ready for the unexpected and prepared to provide for yourselves.

The best way to ensure your own safety and well being is to take responsibility for your own emergency preparedness.

Even if you do not have designated emergency duties, you may be expected to carry out your job functions in an emergency. Other conditions at your workplace or in your community also could make it difficult for you to get home right away. Your family should have plans and resources to take care of themselves in your absence.

Fortunately, there are practical steps you can take now that can make a big difference in a wide range of emergencies:

BE INFORMED
MAKE A PLAN
BUILD A KIT
GET INVOLVED

Be Informed

www.ready.gov/be-informed

Being informed about what might happen is the first step in preparing for an emergency.

Knowing what to do before, during, and after an emergency is a critical part of being prepared, and it may make all the difference when seconds count. Emergencies in the workplace may include natural hazards such as tornadoes or earthquakes, or man-made incidents like hazmat spills, chemical or biological hazards, bomb threats, an active shooter, or workplace violence.

Identify how you can get information from local authorities during an emergency and how you will stay informed. Methods of getting emergency information vary within the National Capital Region (NCR); these include local radio and television, text message alerts, and NOAA Weather Radio alerts. In some cases, you might hear a special siren, get a telephone call, or emergency workers may go door-to-door.

Learn how to receive emergency alerts at work, and know what to do when an announcement is made.

Emergency Text Alerts
www.capitalert.gov

The local governments in the NCR maintain Web sites that allow you to register e-mail addresses, cell phones, and pagers to receive emergency text alerts.

Sign up for emergency alerts from the local communities where you work and where you live, and encourage the rest of your family to sign up, too. Be sure to register an e-mail address or cell phone that you can access during the workday.

- Visit **www.capitalert.gov** for links to the local government alert systems in the NCR.

- Check with the schools, day care facilities, and assisted living centers you visit or use to see if they offer an emergency alert system.

- Public transportation providers also offer alerts on closures and delays.

- Get information from social media sites like Twitter and Facebook. (See page 26 for links to additional resources.)

- Find alternative ways to inform family members who do not have access to electronic devices.

NOAA Weather Radio
www.weather.gov/nwr
Frequency 162.450 WNG736

NOAA Weather Radio All Hazards (NWR) is a nationwide network of radio stations broadcasting continuous weather information

and other emergency alerts directly from the nearest National Weather Service office. NWR broadcasts official Weather Service warnings, watches, forecasts, and other hazard information 24 hours a day, 7 days a week.

NWR broadcasts warnings for all types of hazards, including natural (such as earthquakes or avalanches), environmental (such as chemical releases or oil spills), and public safety (such as AMBER alerts or 911 telephone outages).

Capital Region Updates
www.capitalregionupdates.gov

The jurisdictions of the NCR have developed a new Web portal to communicate emergency information to residents.

Through this online resource, residents can stay connected to local jurisdictional news (through a combined RSS feed of local news releases), local weather from the National Weather Service, traffic and transit alerts, tips on how to prepare for emergencies, and more.

During a regional emergency or major weather event across the NCR, the site will feature incident updates and life-safety news and instructions. It serves as an online "one stop shop" for information and guidance. Visit the site and bookmark it today.

Emergencies at Work

Every workplace is unique, so familiarize yourself with the plans and procedures at your agency, including the notification methods your agency uses to issue emergency alerts and keep employees informed.

Ask your supervisor for more information about the procedures at your specific location so you will know what to do in different situations, from a medical emergency in the office to a major incident in the region.

Supervisors are responsible for ensuring their employees are informed of workplace emergency procedures, and they play a critical role in accounting for employees during drills and actual events.

Protective Actions

In most emergencies affecting an office building, it either will be safer to go outside the building (evacuate) or remain inside (shelter-in-place). If you are told to evacuate or shelter-in-place, follow those instructions immediately.

- If you need to evacuate your building, follow your emergency procedures and directions from emergency personnel. Make sure you know two evacuation routes from your workstation and where to assemble outside.

- Some emergencies, such as severe weather, the release of a hazardous material outside the building, or the threat of a chemical, biological, or radiological attack, may require the opposite of evacuation: remaining inside in an attempt to avoid exposure to dangerous conditions outside. In these situations, "sheltering-in-place," which means staying inside your building or going to a designated safe area, may be the best way to avoid harm.

In most situations, if you are not in immediate danger, your default action should be to **stay where you are** and get more information.

Some sample procedures for evacuation and sheltering-in-place are provided here for your reference. However, every workplace is unique, so be sure to talk to your supervisor about the emergency procedures at your specific location.

Sample Evacuation Procedures

1. **Lock your computer terminal** and quickly secure your work materials.

2. **Take personal possessions** (such as keys, purse, or wallet) with you if you have time, but do not risk your safety by returning to the office to get them.

3. **Leave without delay.** Walk, don't run.

4. **Alert others to the emergency**, and ask if they need help. Account for any visitors and guide them out.

5. **Follow the nearest safe exit route.** If it is obstructed or filled with smoke, use an alternate route.

6. **Stay to the right** in stairwells so emergency personnel can ascend the stairs as you are evacuating. Do not use elevators unless instructed to do so by emergency personnel.

7. **Go to your emergency assembly point**, and check in with your supervisor or other designated point of contact.

Sample Shelter-in-Place Procedures

Your workplace should have specific places identified as shelter-in-place locations, such as interior halls, conference rooms, offices, or storage rooms. Be sure you know at least two such locations.

1. **Move promptly to the designated safe area** in your building, closing office doors behind you.

2. **Grab your emergency preparedness kit** and other personal belongings (like your ID, keys, purse, medication, etc.) if they are readily available, but do not return to the office to get them.

3. **Alert others** to the emergency, and ask if they need help.

4. Use what you have on hand to **maintain a barrier between yourself and any dangerous conditions outside**. For example, for a chemical release, this could mean sealing doors, windows, and vents; for severe weather, this could mean moving to a lower floor or interior part of the building, away from glass and flying debris.

5. **Await further guidance** from building management, security personnel, or the Occupant Emergency Team.

Generally, you only will be asked to shelter-in-place at work until the threat can be assessed, emergency response personnel arrive,  and the dangerous conditions pass. It may take authorities some time to provide information on what is happening, so remain calm and be patient. Even if it appears there is no longer a hazard, continue to shelter-in-place until building management or security personnel issue an "all clear."

See Something, Say Something

If you see something suspicious, say something to security personnel or local law enforcement. Keen awareness of your surroundings could prevent an incident from occurring or give responders valuable information during an emergency.

Make sure the emergency numbers for law enforcement or security personnel are posted next to your phone at work and programmed into your cell phone.

Fire and Emergency Medical Services

Your building may have specific procedures for calling the fire department or emergency medical services beyond simply calling 9-1-1. A large campus or secure building may have procedures in which security personnel escort emergency responders.

Remember that the emergency number may not always be 9-1-1; it may be a different number based on your building's emergency response procedure.

If your building has a nurse or medical staff, know how to call for their assistance. Learn the location of emergency supplies, such as fire extinguishers, alarm pull stations, automated external defibrillators (AEDs), and first aid kits.

Guidance for Specific Hazards

This page provides some general guidance on how to respond to different types of emergencies. Every workplace is unique, however, so talk to your supervisor about the emergency procedures at your specific location. During an actual emergency, be sure to follow the guidance of local public safety officials.

Earthquake

If you are inside:

- Drop to the floor and take cover under a sturdy piece of furniture.
- Hold on until the shaking stops.

If you are outside:

- Stay outside and away from buildings or structures that could collapse or generate falling debris.
- Do not re enter buildings until advised that it is safe to do so.

Medical Emergencies

- Check the scene to make sure it is safe before attempting to help.
- Call 9 1 1 or other workplace emergency number. Provide your exact location and other information about the situation.
- Have someone locate first aid supplies and the Automated External Defibrillator (AED), if available.
- Care for the victim if you are trained, and stay there until help arrives.

Bomb Threat (via telephone)

- Write down the exact wording of the threat.
- If available, follow the directions on your bomb threat reference card.
- Immediately notify building security.
- Follow instructions from building management and/or security personnel.

Chemical Release Outside

- Take shelter inside immediately (many chemicals are colorless and odorless).
- If you were directly exposed to a hazardous chemical, remove and discard any contaminated clothing.
- Remain sheltered until additional information is available.
- Follow guidance from local officials on seeking medical treatment. If you do not believe you have been exposed, let first responders treat the critically injured first.

Power Outage or Blackout

- Remain where you are if it is safe to do so. Do not leave work unless you have a way to get home safely.
- Follow guidance from OPM or other designated officials for information on office closures.
- If traffic lights, trains, and other transit systems are without power, expect extended delays.

Nuclear or Radiological Incident

- Remember three factors: time, distance, and shielding. Try to decrease the time you are exposed to radiation, increase your distance from the contaminated area, and increase the shielding between yourself and any radiation.
- Take shelter in an interior room immediately.
- Discard contaminated clothing and shower as soon as possible.

Workplace Violence

If there is an active shooter:

- Evacuate the building, leave your belongings, and keep your hands visible.
- Hide out of view and block entry to your hiding place.
- Take action as a last resort to attempt to incapacitate the shooter.

Severe Weather - Snow

- Check the National Weather Service for storm advisories, watches, and warnings.
- Only drive if necessary. Allow extra time, and make sure you have a full tank of gas.
- Keep blankets and other emergency supplies in your car in case you get stranded.

Severe Weather - Tornado

- Take shelter immediately.
- Move to an interior room away from windows.
- If you are driving, do not attempt to outrun the tornado. Pull over and seek shelter.
- If you are outside and unable to take shelter inside a structure, lay down in a ditch or low area.

Severe Weather - Hurricane

- Check the National Weather Service for storm advisories, watches, and warnings.
- Before you leave your office, take any items you will need to telework.
- Follow evacuation orders that are issued and do not return to the affected area until advised that it is safe to do so.

For more detailed information on what to do before, during, and after different types of emergencies, visit **www.ready.gov.**

Evacuating the Area vs. Staying Put

Depending on your circumstances and the nature of the emergency, your first important decision is whether to stay where you are or evacuate the area. You should understand and plan for both possibilities.

In many situations, your best initial action is to **stay safe in your home or office building** and wait for more information, instead of trying to evacuate the area and then getting stuck in traffic or exposing yourself to dangerous conditions outside.

Use common sense and available information to determine if there is any immediate danger. If you have time, try to find official guidance before making your own decision. Watch TV, listen to the radio, or check the Internet often for emergency instructions from local officials.

Area-Wide Evacuation

During an emergency, Federal agencies may close their facilities, but area-wide evacuation orders typically will come from the governor, mayor, or county official for the jurisdiction where the evacuation will take place.

If evacuation orders are issued for a wide area, normal transportation systems may be disrupted. Roads may be closed, transit options may be limited, and traffic congestion may choke major evacuation routes from your location.

To get evacuation instructions and determine the best route, tune into local media broadcasts, sign up for local e-mail and text alerts, and visit the Web sites for transit agencies and your local office of emergency management.

(Links to additional resources are provided on page 26.)

Evacuation Routes for the District of Columbia

www.72hours.dc.gov

In the event of an emergency affecting the District of Columbia, a portion of the city could be instructed to evacuate. The D.C. Government has developed specific evacuation routes for each area of the city.

Prior to an emergency, visit **www.72hours.dc.gov** and input your address to create a personalized evacuation map.

If an evacuation requires residents from Maryland or Virginia to leave the region, specific transportation and route information will be provided by local emergency management officials. It is important for all area residents, including those living in Maryland and Virginia, to prepare for a potential evacuation.

If evacuation orders are issued, pay close attention to what areas are affected. Any evacuation will be difficult. **If you are not in harm's way, it may be better for you and others if you remain in place.**

Public Transportation Options

Regardless of whether you normally drive to work or use public transportation, plan alternate ways to get where you need to go in case something happens on your normal route.

- Plan an alternate route from the next closest bus or rail line in case the station or line you normally use is unavailable. (For example, if you normally use the New Carrollton Metro station on the Orange Line, chart an alternate route from the Addison Road station on the Blue Line, or the Greenbelt station on the Green Line.)

- Learn your bus routes. If rail service is unavailable, a bus may get you where you need to go (but anticipate delays due to heavy traffic).

- If you ride Metro, visit **www.wmata.com** or call **(202) 637-7000** for service status or to plan a route home.

- To report an emergency, suspicious activity, or unattended packages in the Metro system, call Metro Transit Police at **(202) 962-2121**. If you ride Metro regularly, save this number in your cell phone.

- Think about alternative transportation, such as biking, walking, or carpooling with coworkers.

Remember that public transportation may not be available during an emergency. Staying at your home or office may be your best option until the emergency is resolved and service is restored.

If the only option is to leave, have a backup plan if all transit services are unavailable. Keep a pair of comfortable walking shoes and a map of the local area at work.

Operating Status of the Federal Government

In an emergency, the U.S. Office of Personnel Management (OPM) will consult with regional authorities and then determine the operating status of the Federal Government in the Washington, D.C. area. OPM will keep the public updated through TV, radio, print, Web sites, and social media.

To the extent possible, OPM will make dismissal and closure announcements prior to the beginning of the workday. This helps reduce morning traffic, and also lessens the commuting burden later in the day if weather conditions deteriorate and OPM announces an early release policy.

In some situations, each agency has the authority and responsibility to take immediate action to protect employees from imminent danger without approval from OPM. Examples include fires, localized flooding or power outages, loss of water, a gas leak, or building damage after an earthquake.

In December 2011, OPM announced three new policies to promote the continuity of government and ensure the safety of Federal employees and the general public. The three new options include:

- **Staggered Early Departure with Final Departure Time:** Federal employees should depart a specified number of hours earlier than their normal departure time, and may request unscheduled leave to depart prior to their scheduled departure time.

- **Shelter-in-Place:** Federal offices in the Washington, D.C. area are under shelter-in-place procedures.

- **Immediate Departure:** Federal employees should depart work immediately.

For the latest information on the Federal Government operating status, visit **www.opm.gov/status**, call **(202) 606-1900**, or visit the official OPM social media pages:

- www.facebook.com/usopm
- www.twitter.com/usopm

Telework and Human Resources Options

Human resources options may be available to assist Federal employees affected by severe weather conditions or other emergencies. This may include leave flexibilities, alternate work schedules, telework prior to an evacuation order, and evacuation assistance.

Telework is an important tool for agencies to continue operations when Federal offices are closed to the public, including during emergency situations, adverse weather conditions, natural disasters, and other incidents that disrupt government operations.

It is important that the Federal Government remain in operation even if offices are closed to the public. "Unscheduled telework" is a relatively new flexibility that allows more Federal employees to work from home, to the extent practicable, when severe weather conditions or other circumstances disrupt or prevent employees from commuting or reporting to work.

For more information on telework or other human resources policies, visit **www.telework.gov** or **www. opm.gov**.

Make A Plan

www.ready.gov/make-a-plan

What would you and your family do if your daily routines were disrupted by an emergency? Do you have a plan?

You and your family may not be together when an emergency occurs, so it is important to agree on what your default actions would be if an emergency affects communication, delays transportation from work or school, or causes your home or neighborhood to be unsafe.

For example, discuss:

- How would you communicate if there were no cell phone service?

- Where would you meet if you could not get home safely?

Plan on How to Communicate

If an emergency occurs while you are at work, you may not have the time or means to contact your family right away.

If traditional landline or cell phone systems are overloaded, consider the following alternate means of communication:

- **Try sending a text message** from your cell phone. It may go through even when you cannot make a call. Make sure all family members know how to send and receive a text if they have a cell phone.

- **Use social media sites** like Facebook or Twitter to get information or update your status.

- **List yourself as safe and well** at **www.safeandwell.org** (sponsored by the American Red Cross).

Consider a plan where each family member calls, e-mails, or sends a text message to the same **out-of-town friend or relative**. It may be easier to make a long distance phone call than to call across town, so an out-of-town contact may be in the best position to communicate among separated family members.

Your department or agency also may have a number to call to check in or receive emergency instructions.

Plan on Where to Meet

Make sure your family knows where to meet after an emergency. You should discuss and agree on **two** family meeting locations:

- One place **in your neighborhood**, in case of a localized emergency (such as a house fire), and
- One place **outside your neighborhood**, such as a relative's house (in case you cannot return home or must evacuate the area).

Make sure each family member has a plan to get to your family meeting spots. Then complete an **emergency contact card** for each family member that identifies emergency contacts and your meeting locations. Each family member should keep the card handy in a wallet, purse, briefcase, or backpack.

For a sample contact card template, visit **www.ready.gov**.

Schools, Day Care, and Assisted Living Centers

During a typical workday, you may be at work, but your other family members may be at school, a day care center, or an assisted living center. Ask how these institutions will communicate their actions with family members or caregivers in an emergency.

- Are there situations in which the facility might be locked down?
- If the facility is evacuated, where will your children or other family members go?
- Can you supply a kit with emergency items specifically for your family member?

Make sure these institutions know how to contact you in an emergency. Prepare a list of family members or caregivers who are authorized to pick up your children in an emergency if you are unavailable.

Tailor Your Plan

Each person's needs and abilities are unique, but everyone can take important steps to prepare for all kinds of emergencies. As you prepare, tailor your plan to your specific daily living needs and responsibilities.

If an emergency occurs during the workday, you may not be able to care for children, pets, or others who depend on you. Create a network of neighbors, relatives, friends, and coworkers who can assist each other in an emergency. Most people have specific personal needs as well as resources to assist others.

Emergency Personnel

If you are a first responder or have other duties in an emergency, you play a critical role in preserving lives, protecting property, or providing other essential services. When you know your family is safe, you will be able to turn your full attention to your mission. Keep in mind:

- Communicating with loved ones may be difficult.

- You may be working in stressful conditions for extended periods of time. You may be required to work extra shifts without knowing the status of your family or the condition of your home or other property.

- Lack of preparedness at home will impact your ability to do your job effectively and safely. Preparing with your family ahead of time will reduce stress and uncertainty on all of you.

For more information, visit **www.ready.gov/responder/**.

Infants and Children

Remember the unique needs of your family when preparing your emergency plan.

Households with infants should plan to have appropriate food and other supplies. Infants' needs change dramatically in very short periods of time, so be sure to update your plan every few months.

If you have children, learn the emergency plans at their day care or school. Try to make emergency planning fun for children by visiting **www.ready.gov/kids/**.

People with Disabilities or Access/Functional Needs

- Make sure you can receive emergency alerts in an accessible form.

- Consider how a disaster might affect your individual needs. Think about the services, items, and devices you use on a daily basis, which may include medications, communications tools, medical equipment, assistive technology, a service animal, or other transportation or health-related items.

- Plan to make it on your own, at least for a period of time. You may not have access to a medical facility or even a drugstore.

- Create your own personal support network by identifying others who will help you. Consider family, friends, neighbors, and faith-based and community groups, and tell these people where you keep your emergency supplies and how they can assist you.

- If you receive life-sustaining medical treatment, identify the location of more than one facility, and work with your provider to develop your own personal emergency plan.

- During an evacuation at work, there may be designated assembly areas for personnel who cannot evacuate down stairs. Check on the procedures at your workplace, and make sure you can access designated shelter-in-place locations.

Additional resources for people with disabilities are available at **www.disability.gov**.

Pets

Whether you decide to stay put in an emergency or evacuate to a safer location, you need to make plans in advance for your pets.

If you evacuate your home, take your pets with you. However, if you are going to a public shelter, understand that pets may not be allowed inside. Plan for alternatives that will work for both you and your pets. Consider friends outside the area who would be willing to host you and your pets in an emergency.

In addition, make sure you have:

- Pet food, medications, bottled water, and other pet supplies

- A current photo of you and your pet for identification purposes

- A secure pet carrier, leash, or harness for your pet

- Up-to-date identification tags securely fastened to your pet's collar

- Your pet's vaccination records, which may be critical for admission into shelters that allow pets

For more information or to see a short video, visit **www.ready.gov/animals/**.

Build A Kit

www.ready.gov/build-a-kit

An emergency preparedness kit is simply a collection of basic items you may need during an emergency. Take a moment to assemble a kit now. When an emergency occurs, you probably will not have time to search or shop for the supplies you need.

You should be prepared to survive on your own after an emergency. This means having your own food, water, and other supplies in sufficient quantity to last for at least **three days**. In addition, basic services such as electricity, gas, water, sewage treatment, and telephones may be unavailable for days or even weeks. Your kit should contain items to help you manage during these outages.

At Home

Recommended items include:

- ❑ Water (one gallon per person per day for at least three days, for drinking and sanitation)
- ❑ Food (at least a three-day supply of non-perishable food)
- ❑ Manual can opener for food
- ❑ Battery-powered or hand-crank radio and a NOAA Weather Radio with tone alert (and extra batteries for both)
- ❑ Flashlight with extra batteries
- ❑ First aid kit
- ❑ Whistle (to signal for help)
- ❑ Dust mask (to help filter contaminated air)

- ❏ Maps of the local area
- ❏ Cell phone charger, inverter, or solar charger
- ❏ Important documents (such as copies of insurance policies, identification and proof of address, financial records, list of allergies or known medical conditions, and emergency contact information)

Additional items than can be useful:

- ❏ Prescription medications and an extra pair of glasses
- ❏ Infant formula and diapers
- ❏ Pet food and extra water for your pet
- ❏ Extra cash
- ❏ Extra clothing, including a long-sleeved shirt, long pants, and sturdy shoes
- ❏ Feminine supplies and personal hygiene items
- ❏ Moist towelettes, garbage bags, and plastic ties for personal sanitation
- ❏ Duct tape and plastic sheeting
- ❏ Wrench or pliers to turn off utilities
- ❏ Work gloves
- ❏ Matches in a waterproof container
- ❏ Books, games, puzzles, or other activities for children

Assemble these items in one place and keep your kit where it is easily accessible. Your items should be stored in a container that is easy to find and easy to carry. If one big container is too difficult to move, consider two smaller containers.

At Work

You also should keep a kit of basic emergency supplies at work. Be sure your kit is accessible and has the items you will need if you have to shelter-in-place.

Suggested items include:

- ❏ Water and non-perishable food
- ❏ Change of clothing
- ❏ Comfortable walking shoes
- ❏ Prescription medications
- ❏ Personal hygiene items
- ❏ Rain gear
- ❏ Flashlight
- ❏ Battery-powered or hand-crank radio
- ❏ First aid kit
- ❏ Whistle (to attract attention)
- ❏ Dust mask (to help filter contaminated air)
- ❏ Copies of important documents (such as insurance and medical information)
- ❏ Emergency contact information

You also may want to include a map of the local area. Even if you know the area around your office fairly well, in an emergency, you may find yourself looking for resources you do not normally use at work.

Consider keeping all your items in a large, airtight plastic bag so the contents can stay clean, dry, and free from harmful contaminants. Be sure your emergency supplies will be ready when you need them.

In Your Car

If you have a car, you also should keep a kit of basic emergency supplies in your vehicle. Consider some of the same items you have in your emergency kits at home and work, such as water, non-perishable food, a first aid kit, and a flashlight with extra batteries. You also may want to include jumper cables, flares, and a car cell phone charger.

If winter weather is forecasted, consider adding a warm blanket, ice scraper, shovel, and sand or grit for traction.

If your vehicle becomes stuck, be aware that carbon monoxide can build up in the vehicle if the engine is running and the exhaust pipe becomes blocked by snow.

Starter Kits

If the idea of putting together an emergency preparedness kit seems like a daunting task, you may want to consider buying a pre-packaged starter kit. Many kits can be purchased pre-assembled from a number of non-profit organizations and local retailers. However, whether purchasing a starter kit or assembling your own, be sure to customize your kit to meet your own individual needs.

Maintaining Your Kits

After you have assembled your kits, be sure to check them **twice a year** and replace expired or outdated items. Check batteries and expiration dates of food, water, and medication. A good time to do this is each spring and fall, when you set your clocks forward or back for Daylight Saving Time.

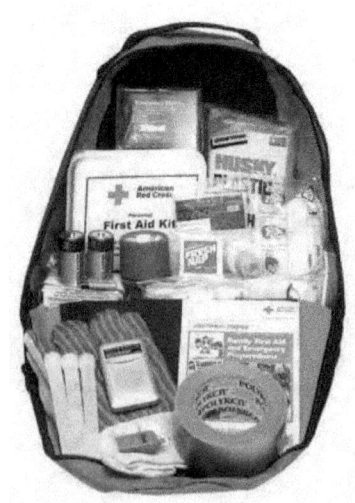

Get Involved

www.ready.gov/get-involved

You can play an active role in making your home, workplace, or community safer and more resilient. For example:

- Volunteer to join your building's Occupant Emergency Team or other emergency organization.

- Take a CPR or first aid class.

- Take free online training from FEMA's Emergency Management Institute at **www. training.fema.gov/is/**.

- Volunteer to support disaster efforts in your community. Get trained and volunteer with a Community Emergency Response Team (CERT), Medical Reserve Corps unit,

or Citizen Corps partner or affiliate organization.

- Join or support volunteer organizations like the American Red Cross in the National Capital Region or other community or faith-based organizations.

Visit **www.citizencorps.gov** and enter your Zip code to find programs in your local community, or visit **www. redcrossnca.org** for opportunities with the American Red Cross in the National Capital Region.

Be sure to affiliate yourself with an organization and get the necessary training **before** your help is needed in a disaster.

Additional Resources

Visit **www.training.fema.gov/is/** to access this preparedness information in a free online course, IS-450.NC: *Emergency Preparedness for Federal Employees in the National Capital Region* (approx. 60 minutes)

Federal Emergency Management Resources

- Are You Ready? An In-Depth Guide to Citizen Preparedness: www.ready.gov/are-you-ready-guide
- Centers for Disease Control and Prevention: www.emergency.cdc.gov
- Citizen Corps: www.citizencorps.gov
- FEMA: www.fema.gov
- Flu Guidance: www.flu.gov
- Ready: www.ready.gov
- U.S. Office of Personnel Management: www.opm.gov

State Emergency Management Resources

- District of Columbia: www.hsema.dc.gov
- Maryland: www.mema.maryland.gov
- Virginia: www.vaemergency.gov

Regional Resources

- American Red Cross - National Capital Region: www.redcrossnca.org
- Capitalert: www.capitalert.gov
- Metropolitan Washington Council of Governments: www.mwcog.org
- NCR News and Information: www.capitalregionupdates.gov

Social Media Resources

Twitter: www.twitter.com/

- DC_HSEMA
- FEMA
- MDMEMA
- RedCrossNCR
- USOPM
- VDEM
- WMATA

Facebook: www.facebook.com/

- LoudounCountyRedCross
- HSEMADC
- FEMA
- MDMEMA
- MWCOG
- USOPM
- VAemergency

Preparedness Checklist

- ☐ Sign up for emergency alerts at **www.capitalert.gov**.

- ☐ Visit **www.capitalregionupdates.gov** and bookmark the site.

- ☐ Visit **www.weather.gov/nwr/** for information on NOAA Weather Radio.

- ☐ Familiarize yourself with your building's Occupant Emergency Plan (OEP) or other workplace emergency plan.

- ☐ Know at least two shelter-in-place locations at work.

- ☐ Know two evacuation routes from work and where to assemble outside.

- ☐ Post the emergency numbers for law enforcement or security personnel next to your phone at work, and program them into your cell phone.

- ☐ Visit **www.72hours.dc.gov** and input your address to create a personalized evacuation map for the District of Columbia.

- ☐ If you normally drive to work, learn alternate routes home, and be prepared to walk or take public transportation. If you normally use public transportation, learn alternate routes, lines, and service providers.

- ☐ To report an emergency, suspicious activity, or unattended packages in the Metro system, call Metro Transit Police at **(202) 962-2121**.

- ☐ For the latest information on the Federal Government operating status, visit **www.opm.gov/status/** or call **(202) 606-1900**.

- ☐ Pick two family meeting locations: one right outside your home, and one outside your neighborhood. Make sure each family member has a plan to get to your family meeting spots.

- ☐ Choose an out-of-town friend or relative that all family members will contact if separated.

- ☐ Be sure all family members know how to send a cell phone text message.

- ☐ Prepare a family emergency contact list with the numbers and e-mail addresses for friends, neighbors, caregivers, and schools.

- ☐ Ask about the emergency plans in place at the schools, day care centers, or assisted living centers you visit or use.

- ☐ Build a kit of basic emergency supplies for home and work.

- ☐ Keep basic emergency supplies in your car.

- ☐ Get involved! Play an active role preparing your home, workplace, or community, and see how you can volunteer to help after a disaster.